Strangers in Light Coats

SEAGULL
BOOKS
•
CELEBRATING
40 YEARS

THE ARAB LIST

ALSO AVAILABLE BY **THE AUTHOR**

Describing the Past
Translated by Samuel Wilder

Where the Bird Disappeared
Translated by Samuel Wilder

An Old Carriage with Curtains
Translated by Samuel Wilder

RECENT TITLES IN **THE ARAB LIST**

SINAN ANTOON
Postcards from the Underworld
Translated by the Author

SALIM BARAKAT
Come, Take a Gentle Stab
Translated by Huda Fakhreddine and Jayson Iwen

RAMY AL-ASHEQ
Ever Since I Did Not Die
Translated by Isis Nusair

GHASSAN ZAQTAN

Strangers in Light Coats

Selected Poems, 2014–2020

TRANSLATED BY ROBIN MOGER

LONDON NEW YORK CALCUTTA

The Arab List
SERIES EDITOR
Hosam Aboul-Ela

Seagull Books, 2023

Text © Ghassan Zaqtan, 2023

First published in English translation by Seagull Books, 2023
English translation © Robin Moger, 2023

ISBN   978 1 8030 9 238 6

British Library Cataloguing-in-Publication Data
A catalogue record for this book is available from the British Library

Typeset by Seagull Books, Calcutta, India
Printed and bound by WordsWorth India, New Delhi, India

RAMALLAH

CONTENTS

I Do Not Know the Way to Aleppo

Sara, take my hand . . .

Sara, take my hand,
I am blind and do not see.
   I think to cry each time the scent of cropped herbs
stirs in your palm.

Herb gatherer, take my hand,
I am young and do not know,
   and my legs go giddy
      when you bend over me
      and without meaning it your loose breasts rock before my eye.

I do not know the way to Aleppo

Sara, take my hand,
Mother sleeps and Father's taken by the river
and I have no dream to dream.
The weavers took my brothers to Aleppo
and left me here to tell my mother when she wakes
  that the river took my father,
    and the weavers took my brothers,
  and that she is dead.

Sara, take my hand.
Night has come,
the day is now behind us,
  and I do not know the way to Aleppo.

As I gathered your firewood and lit you fire on the Sabbath

Jewish Sara,
as you pass beneath the olives on the mountains' slopes and shoulders,
   down the links of low stone walls laid out by village women's hands,
call to me and I will come out to you from the shadows
   in your Arab eyes;
      invoke my name and scale its thousand articulations.

Alone in this dark we stare and do not see; there is
no star to guide us,
no staff on which to lean
   and wave away the snakes in these hills,
no road to take.

I have no home
and you have no exile.

Six brothers and I am their seventh;
I have no sisters.

The guides led the caravans to the deserts
and left their longing on the fences.
The guides, your dead guests:
no trace of them in the dust,
no news of them in the houses.

As you turn in your sleep, the old horses fret in the yards, and the carts,
   abandoned by the roadsides, sigh,
      and the poets who have lost the markers of their pedigree, sigh.

The mules alone climb the mountain-face, a brigade
  victorious and dead.

You are sleeping and I am thinking of you,
and at night I unpick my threads from your carpet,
  and in vain.

It was something that happened,
  not a prophecy.

In the twilight, the abandoned forms of the trees and houses fade,
the exiles whistle in their beds,
and the wind that gathers in their nightmares roars
while you turn in your sleep
and the dry leaves crackle beneath the feet of the slain warriors.

Did you hear the whisper of the leaves crawling
and murmuring in the woods,
and did they gleam,
the eyes of the dead in your dreams,
  on the Sabbath,
as I gathered your firewood and lit you fire?

No light to guide your way, no birthmark to guide my mother to me

Christian Sara,
I have no light to guide your way
and no birthmark to guide my mother to me.

The boys have gone to the valleys,
the women have left the bread in the dirt,
   and the centurion has hauled the men off by their necks
and closed the roads to Bethlehem.

The screams of the hermits slaughtered on the rocks and slopes of Wadi Qelt
came in one morning, after seven days and nights
mixed with the shouts of the Persian troops,
the reek of their blood laid on the low thresholds of the Christians' houses
   by the wind.

Take me with you to the stonecutters' hills;
I shall gather you straw so you might sleep at night,
and calm your heart by singing down the mountain trails.

Take me with you: you are afraid
   and my voice is beautiful.

Your road is long and my stars are good

No raisins in my saddlebags nor dates.
The shepherds abandoned me, the foxes turned their backs on me,
and there was no water, no bed, no blanket.
The caves in the hillside shut their eyes
  and I had no guide.
The hyenas caught my scent and the wolves howled on my trail.
Mute on my path of prophecy, and you are calling to me
the names of your children
and laying charms and talismans.

The cold pricks my body like needles; no sleep comes
and hyena thirst circles me; I follow it
  sleepwalking to its lair.
The shepherds took my name and portioned it between them
  like a butchered beast
and you are searching on my body for a mark.

Sara, take my hand.
Take me with you to Mecca.
Your road is long
  and my stars are good.

While you slept on straw

While you slept on straw
I watered your horse and fed it; I washed it
and rubbed its taut hide with my shirt.

As the sweat shone, studded on your breasts,
    and rolled like marbles down the passageway that tilts in your sleep,
I lullabied your child, who saw everything.
The voices of the woodcutters were coming from the trees
and along the hill-line their hungry daughters
    set snares for deer
    and traps for the village boys who,
while they were shouting like dogs in heat, I was crawling
like a blind snake, tumbling like a pebble
    picked by your fingers from the river's flux,
and my lips were picking out the needles of straw caught in your tangled hair
    and stuck to your thighs and breasts,
        straw by straw,
                like a bird pecks bread.

When that happens

When things grow thin and the shadows trapped
in their strict forms come apart
and the djinn begin to scale the gardens' fences and the bougainvillea
and slip through the intimate arrangement of the cactus pads,

When he sees them with his own eyes, the djinn,
sprawled on the doorsteps of the houses,
over the minaret's crescent and dawn's dewed prayers and supplications,

When a djinn calls his name from the wooden shelf
in his mother's room, his mother
whose features lately he cannot quite recall,
which causes him pain, which sends his way a fear that troubles him,

When the lepers who hung from the trees in the woods climb down
and their scared eyes glitter in the oak groves on the slopes, those
    he encountered in a Christian novel he could not recall
                                    how it had come to his library,

When they are liberated from the book, from the riddle of the miracle,
    and start to roam
        like open suitcases down the lanes of nearby villages
with faces uncovered and smiles that are hard to believe,

When their feet touch earth and they pick up stones,
    only because these remember their distant childhoods
    and their cracked fingers
        furrowed by the curse,

When he hears his dog's monotonous barking
   coming as though from wells abandoned
in the hidden foothills of memories, his dog
who has limped wounded along the riverbank
since the soldiers killed it there thirty years ago.

When the new houses on the mountain disappear
   into the twilight
      with the construction sites and cranes, haphazard
      cabins of the workmen and guards,
and a single light remains whose source he cannot see,
   like a secret spring pulling off its mask to breathe,

When he sees the dead trees and the trees
   uprooted by the dozers, the woodcutters' saws, the muffled hatchets,
   rising from the furrows,
      beginning to gather up their branches
         with the sureness of the dead, with a ghost's mistrust,
      rising from their fabricated forms—
the seats in the sittings rooms, benches in the parks,
the shelves and desks in offices, austere cafe chairs;
   from the cupboards, leaving the clothes suspended in air like
      bodies upheld without hope—
and walking to the mountain,
a happy family
coming home from the masquerade.

When he sees the children,
   forgotten by the dead patrols and the betrayed columns,
   and the cries caught in night's snares,
      crossing, exhausted, the cold dark of the mountain,
         the damp dark of the fields,
to the dark of the homes they have missed,

he knows in his heart,
in a way of which he knows nothing,
that he has reached his land.

It rains in the short and tree-lined street

Down the short and tree-lined street I come
from Restaurant Anglo to The Baladiya
where I saw Edward Said for the first time,
leaning on Ibrahim Abu Lughd, when
    it was raining beneath

    beneath their slow advance along the short and tree-lined street
it was raining on the novel, on the old cloth covering
    the children, abandoned in the holed boats, on those
stood in the alley, the woman
in a man's overcoat, the man who sinks
his head in his hands, leaning on the window after midnight.

It rained without stopping, it was
prophesying, lightning-and-thundering
on the tombstones and the lighthouses,
on the courtiers and the priests and the poets,
on the speakers in the public squares, the judges,
the actors, the new imams and the preachers,
the drowned children,
the newborn girl buried alive.

It rained on those waiting for the barbarians, on the barbarians
who came almost immediately after the poem's end
and set up their tents on the cliff-edge.

It rained on the conversation between the two men
  as they went on their way
    beneath the arcs of eucalyptus and the damp pine cones,
and from all directions, from the hills around the town particularly,
could be heard the barbarians' cries, and their fire
could be seen in the night, just as, rain easing,
  one could make out the sighs of their women,
the susurrus of bracelets and anklets, their black hair's swish, their men
breathing, belching in their dreams.

It was raining on the barbarians and on their horses
and on their strange encampment
on the cliff-edge, shortly after the end of the last line
where time lies open, unshepherded, onto the abyss,
outside the chronicles of the priests, the judges' gestures, the celebrations
of the king, the marvels of the actors, the imams' prayers, the preachers'
maxims, the advice of the drowned,
the single question of the newborn buried alive,

when everything, nearly everything, hangs
on the malice of the gods, their machinations,
the guile of their bored daughters.

Nor you nor I

The white come down to the Persian rug from the walls,
the trucks' lights shaking the bed and the shadows,
and there is a whispering from the winter canvas hung on the darkness,
the whisper which in our nightmares lights the woods.

The guards' patrols and their calls worry the grass and the napping birds
and leave the young man hidden in the ditch
like a dead rag.

The woman whose husband rapes her nearly every night
dozes at the window, waiting.
The crying boy, son of our Christian neighbour,
screams behind the mosquito net
as his mother gestures with her two hands at the dark.

The widow looks at the photos and laughs with all her heart.

The light from the only street lamp hits the floor
    and strikes the family portrait.
The few voices scale the fences like anxious, noiseless ghosts.
All outside the beam of light is shadow now.
Objects seem like shadows dried out in the dark.

The man who rapes his wife nearly every night returns from work
and shutters the window.
In the ditch, the young man is curled like a foetus
and there is someone crying out of the shadows.

Our Christian neighbour, mother of the weeping boy,
prays before the netting where her son is
   whimpering in his sleep.
The widow sleeps, uncovered as always;
her breasts breathe in the slantwise light, troubled breathing,
and her knees gleam,
and in the portrait a fat man looks at her,
is laughing like a child.

Do you see?
Nor you, nor I,
in these wilds
can sing alone.

Song of the girl at the fence

Let it happen,
said the traveller to the girl at the fence.

The stranger said to her:
Let the land to walk to its people,
and: Knot your lock
to be happily wed.

And the bird as it flew by:
Daughter,
do not sleep here;
light fire, for the cold rolls the road
behind the hills, like a rug in the wind.

And the soldier:
You would not know me if I returned,
for the war eats those who kill and those who are killed
and nothing comes home but the howl.

And a boy beside her told her:
My father saw me dead in his dream,
so you best keep clear.

And the well said:
Your eyes are of me.

The city without them

What happened to the exiles?
They are not in the parks
or the police stations, or the emergency rooms in the hospitals;
no sign of them at the roadside or in the suburbs' fastnesses.

What has happened to the exiles, wretched ramblers,
with the sapped faces, the poems
preoccupied with yearning and suffering,
who roam the parks aimlessly,
reading old newspapers, studying the weather in places unreachable,
in villages and towns that nobody has heard of?

What has become of the faces that trigger doubts, their hard creeds,
those queer clothes, unfit for climbing stairs, for public transport?
What of their mongrel dictions and beastly whiskers,
their endless errors when walking and boarding and crossing the street,
their stumbling on the escalators in shopping malls and metros,
their smoking, those heads
ducked before women, their elders, the police?

What is happening to the distant homelands that fill their bedroom walls,
their battered wallets, their pitiful and gaudy flags, their anthems
crude and droning, imprisoned in terse phrasing and childish tunes?

What has befallen their grimy boys, the girls in hijab?
What has happened to them, this cold night,
the city so bleak and wild?

The anthem of the statues

Here we are, stumbling in our dreams and rising
to reach the squares on time,

our forms, shaped like the gods',
and our limbs bared
to the passers-by and windows, and the birds
                                        that we hold.

Rhetoric and trickery
and destinies bent like victory arches, too;

in our wake, the crowds
and eloquently expressed designs
and wise plans realized.

The marks left by skilled sculptors
on the ribs on our breasts
and the shoulders' slopes
and the pelvises go on
growing over our bodies
like assiduous vines.

Our loyalties are blind
and our efforts acclaimed.

Our shadows pant on the pavements
while we rise from each fall on our way to the squares to arrive
as destined:

each to their plinth
that was waiting there always;

blind destiny from which
there is no deliverance
and no escape.

The Road to the Lakes

No one believed them

Who reached the lakes (only a few in any case, and many of those pretending)
   said that they (they meant the dead) would come there singly,
      their sighs carried over their arms like blankets from another world.
They also said that they (the dead) were starting to take their memories
from their chests, pips from flesh, and were lining them on the sand,
one by one, to struggle like birds tipped from their cage
      unaided to the water.
Others (less wise) said that they (the dead) were drying their days on the
sand like washed rags or (there were those who said) like furniture faded
from use; that they were beginning to narrate them, clearing the dust
from the dark nooks, from the door handles, from the chair legs, from the
washing on the line, from the window panes and mirrors, the photos from
trips abroad and weddings.
Who reached the lakes said this and more
   and no one believed them.

Asleep in the corridor of the birds

Asleep in the corridor of the birds,
the bushes are leaning in my dream,
  and there is a distant beating of wings yet to arrive;
  I cannot see them, but now I guess where they're going.
They exhausted me, the paths by the lakes that lead nowhere
  but to each other.
If but you knew, in sleep the smell of water has weight,
and at night the cold rises from its cave,
and when we lie alone sleep takes us to a darkness in the mountain.
Here howl wolves invisible,
though in the morning their tracks show plain
  around us.
  Here, we forget;
we pursue the river's trail in a journey set loose by the springs,
but we do not arrive.

Companions of the Kurdish boy

The foxes came with me from the lowland thickets to the foothills,
and a friend of mine, too, who had died in the war in Beirut:
blond, limping in death.
He thought I was Moroccan, from the Rif,
and spoke to me of a friend of his who had gone to Fes
and in Fes had died from love.
I thought he was from the villages of the Kurds in the marches of Iraq.

Someone is going up through the woods

There is someone going up through the woods, said the boy,
breathing hard beneath the blanket.
The cry that at first I'd thought a wolf, that came from the woods,
was the long call of a woman killed in the ruins.
She called to her family from there, in the voice of the dead man,
and at the foot of the hill
the pine and cypress were climbing down to the streets
and the houses
and the water.

We buy strange fruit from sellers we cannot see

It was past midnight,
   said the one who had come from the woods.
      Or later.
We were here
buying strange fruit
   past midnight
from sellers we could not see.

A darkness crossed the cane fields.
There was no time to grasp what was happening or wake the sleepers.

   The houses there were all alike.
   The scream of glass ceased.
Night's edge was rolling down the metalled road.

The great wind ceased,
and time vanished.

Then he said, as though directed,

Your heart, now,
is black.

It wasn't his voice;
   it wasn't any voice.

Leaning as they went beneath the weight of memory

In the woods they would call the names of those who were gone,
  one by one,
and they were swimming, the names,
in the heavy air, conserved in prayer,
and we would see them as they passed along the paths
and by the fences of the houses,
through the ruins where the mules sleep.

And we would see them as they came down the road to the graveyard
of the Muslims, the monastery's graveyard, the muezzin's house, the
unmarked grave of the young woman on the slope of the plain, the
cave of the foxes, the figs round the fountain, the ruins where the figs
grow, the spring of the pigeons, the ruins by the spring, the well of
the stranger, the ruins by the well;
passing through the shadows with no urge to arrive,
with no desire to remain,
and we would toss them our bread so they would see us.

We would see them sitting
singly on the doorsteps of the houses
and by the springs
  white with death,
or climbing, leaning
as they went beneath the weight of memory.

The hymns

The hymns would come from the direction of the river.
The hymns always reminded me of the mist that swells the river,
spilling its ghosts into the fields and irrigation canals.
From the direction of the river the soldiers came and cast their defeat at us.
After them came a column with victory medals.
At the end of the column came many dead men
   returning the hymns' vestments to the river.

The river hymn

River, river,
   take our people north,
help them through the hunger, cold and wind,
take the pictures of the dead and take their bread,
   (the travellers may hunger)
and with them bring their silence in the evenings
when the birds sleep and the keys are working.

River, river,
   when their children cross, be warm,
silk soft, be measured
as the commandments,
charitable as a bridge.

River, river,
   soften your breeze
as the daughters wade the fords into the twin darknesses
   of temptation and patience;
be still as the muezzin's daughter crosses at the ford, be
as a carpet laid out for her by the birds
   as she steps down, out of his voice,
     into the prayers and the dawn.

River, river,
be still when the teacher's daughter crosses;
wet her hair for her so the horses will carry us,
wet her neck for her so the roads see us,

wet her breast for her so that the dove settles on the palm trees,
so the boats might find their way from evening's smooth passage
to the night,

wet her hip for her so we might love to drown.

River,
   wet her palm for her so that the stranger might return,
so the beast and the birds can find their way,
rejoice, because you have brushed that beauty,
and be kind so she may pass.

River, O river:
take her, take us,
and take our people north.

The arrival of the woman whose husband the sniper we killed in the last war

Against the fire's glow we saw a shadow slumbering, a woman on the
hill's slope with no basket or offerings in her hand; I thought
   the hymns had brought her.
In her thirties, dark-skinned or almost so, the cold of the hills, that
you know, was whipping in her wake as it rolled up the road like a
rug in the wind,
and the young man was afraid, and no one was on the road.
   The breach that the two cypresses opened for her stood upright,
like someone watching her as she grew greater in her shadow.
Like that she was standing in the space that the cypresses had made.

She was like us

The woman whose husband the sniper we killed in the last war
was searching, like us, for the road to the lakes.
We shared our bread on the road, and to pass the time
we talked of the dead.

The exhaustion was rising off her heart like a faint smoke
and vanishing into the steaming dew,
and I was watching her as she sighed,
as her shirt opened and between her breasts the hollow shone.
Even on the road to the lakes one can think this way.
   She was guided by the fire and the smell, as she told us later.

She did not describe things well

She shared the loaf with us and pointed us to the lakes.
She was searching for her husband. He died in the war, too.
We killed him in the war, we told her on the road.
And it seemed to me that I heard his voice as he drank his coffee,
telling her his dream,
and that I could see his face beneath the cold on the hills
he never reached, then
the grins of the hyenas
who accompanied him to his sleep,
the footfalls around him
on his way back home,
his obliviousness as he told her, or us, how it had seemed,
or what he had seen behind the mask.

What the sniper told his widow

I see a circle of light, nothing else.
No heart, no sadness, no memories, no shadow.
Just two, alone in the circle of light.
I choose him, just him, without a past or family,
without a woman or land or home to support,
then I hold him a moment, or two,
just him,
alone now in the circle of light,
but he does not see me.

She did not describe things well.

So I go home, to make sure that my fear is safe with me,
and that you are waiting.
Nothing lets me sleep
save you are waiting and the fear.

They walk behind me

At night I hear their footsteps and mine, he tells her as he weeps,
and I recognize them as I walk and they walk behind me;
I order their rhythms on the road and I speak their descriptions
so they might pass,
  so they might go on one by one down the alleys or climb the narrow steps
    darkened by the feet of passers-by and bleached by height.
At their own pace (thus, their obedience) they climb
  at their own pace, like sailors
they climb, the alley their ship, their reproach a pole to the oars, their forms
blowing the wind at windows, at the houses,
their astonishment filling the sail.

Behind the mask I am other than I, I am
become the mask.
I see what the mask sees,
I hear the mask's voice.

All of them, the little girl aside, would come to sit in the living room,
their forms a blur, and stare at the boy's bed,
  which we kept after he died.
The man who brings bags of vegetables would come late,
panting. Would sit with the bags clutched to his chest.
The woman in hijab would try to cover the hole between her eyes.
But the little girl would go and lie in our dead son's bed.

Every day before you wake I start to clean the room.
I sweep away the smoke and dust left by the woman in hijab
and gather the vegetables from the carpet
and clean the blood of the little girl from our boy's bed.

The oars and the trumpet and the bridge

The sound of the oars is carried by the gust of wind out to the frontiers
    and scattered to all corners.
Together we passed through the hillsides of oak to the forest of pines.
She was leaning slightly, and coming towards us out of his voice,
as he was telling stories and drowning in his voice.
As we climbed, I swapped bread with her for memories.

The trumpet

The doves pecked the bread from my basket
and the evening was content with presence.
There is someone blowing the trumpet now,
there is someone guarding the dead and guiding them
    to the deep cracks in the earth
where are the roots.

The bridge

When we rested on the rail of the bridge, she leaned,
as if to avoid a plea from her heart,
or to scatter the butterflies, suddenly arrived and guided
effortlessly to her breast,

and the lakes were behind the hills.

Speak, Stranger, Speak

The solitude of the fortune teller

The birds that were leading me to the springs are not yet here.
Their cry reaches me, trapped in November, one evening
   in a winter that I struggle to recall.
The foxes that were leading me to the mountain passes
that I named for the valleys
have yet to return from their long night.
The signs left by the shepherds and the woodcutters and the deer hunters
to guide their daughters and sturdy wives
   are scattered by the hot winds blowing in from somewhere in the desert.
The children who would climb the hill to see the line of the lakes
   followed the slope of the hillside down before the khamseen could come in.
Only I am left in these wilds,
   watching the winds which move the sands
   and the lakes which dry.

Speak, stranger

Stranger,
O stranger,
for so long that I've stopped remembering,
for days that I no longer count,
no one has come this way.
The lost stopped coming down the darkened tracks,
the outlines of their unquiet forms along the line of the hills
   are there no more.
   Stay a little, stranger,
I shall not ask your name
or where you go; just sit
by the light of the candle I lit for you
so I might remember the form you were, and speak,
speak, stranger, speak, so I might find my voice
taken by the wind that shifts the sands.

To be born in Beit Jala

I was born into the Christian households of Beit Jala,
the spacious stone homes
over the olive presses
where in autumn the heavy millstones turn
and the Arab women cross themselves
as the oil gushes down the runnels and the deep odour curls
      beneath the arches, beneath the decades.

I was born among women
into the stream of hymns,
  when Sundays had the scent of mint tea
    on the Muslim women's balconies,
and between the robes of women fasting and virtue's palisades.
The gift of patience clung to me,
and the bird thoughts which they store beneath their pillows,
and the joyful dispositions that they set loose
into the close air of the villages of the south.

I was born in summer. I bore
the Arab name of a Syrian born in Alawite villages far away
  in the mists of the north.
I would climb with it on my shoulder like a bird,
and descend with it following like a shadow,
and when I slept it would enter my dreams as Me,
which, when I noticed it, would lead me.
I walk after my name and I call to it, and Me turns, nervously.
It was murdered in winter and I was born in summer.

43

It is my name, that I work with to this day.
I took from it
   the miracles of loss
   and the courage of one who does not know,
   and without meaning to I woke it.

I was born at midday,
   peach pickers among the vines.

Seller of the unseen

I am the seller of the unseen, charms and talismans, passer through
your dreams, no home to take him in, no appointment to meet.
If you see him in the marketplace, follow him
so the memories you're yet to make don't go astray.
From a Moroccan magician I took sleight of hand, the trade
of reading faces and preying on the lost.
I would pick them out in the marketplaces and the squares by their
eyes, their vague and puzzled eyes, left behind in distant places, on the
trees of their ruined countries, the fences of their abandoned villages,
the disoriented rivers, tables in coffee shops that drift through their
memories,
a gaze held suspended, clouded in lovers' assignations,
and glances fringed by shynesses and murmurings.
I saw many eyes;
they are my trade.
I stole their fear and pain and sadnesses
and sold it all to strangers who had come to watch.

Guide for the lost and his seven nights

Despite their doubts, their painful experiences with travellers on the road, gypsies guided me until I came to the outskirts of a dusty village whose houses ringed a single tavern like a bracelet rings a wrist.

On the first night
their women gave me a pallet of straw that sighed until the morning star rose, and six coloured beads:
A bead for the road and a bead for the home.
A bead for the one who goes by and a bead for those who stay.
A bead for wisdom and a bead for luck.

On the second night
their young men gave me three short daggers with handles of mock ivory:
A dagger for love,
a dagger for jealousy,
and a dagger for regret.

On the third night
I went out into open country and there were distant lights as though of a lost caravan:
Darkness, O darkness, O
black aunt,
my saddlebags are empty
and my road is desolate;
my country is far away
and my lover has forgotten me.

On the fourth night
I saw Lorca by the light of a smoking candle.
He was seducing a woman on the bank of a river
whose name I have forgotten
and I was cleaning a bull from the lance of a dead matador
whose name as it so happened was Ignacio,
though truth be told I loved Constantine Cavafy more:
his querulous heart, his dimly lit chamber.
We lit incense, left charms in the temples of Antioch, and drank with
a pagan who'd come to Sidon on a merchant ship and knew the
Athenians' poetry by heart,
and we listened to the poets of the Syrian coast and their limpid Greek.

On the fifth night
I read the poets of the Aegean and listened to the storytellers of the
archipelago, the islands' wonders, the boasts of the Spartans, the feats
of the gods,
but I loved Yasser Arafat more:
sprightly and small, with his supple Egyptian twang.
We came from many cities on the Mediterranean coast. We liberated
slaves and altered destinies and built towers and ploughed fallow fields,
and never stayed for long.
We raided the night in its darkness, and followed the sea lanes and the
barges of the mourning women, and we saw the ghost ships which
resemble elegies.
In exile, we made brothers of hyenas,
and we sent messages and messengers to the rainforests in the north,
and we seduced the mountains and the winds,
and we saw everything.

On the sixth night
I left my horse to go alone to Cordoba.

On the seventh night,
my stars read, my purpose manifest, my time here at an end,
I gathered myself and climbed alone the road to Ithaca.

There is nothing left for me to do here

There is nothing left for me do in this town,
nothing left for me to say to the people here:
I am the only carpenter for seven villages which sprout on the lakeshore
  like seven clusters of mushrooms.
For their boys and girls I made many toys, and ploughs for their poor
fields, solid shelving for their women's kitchens, nayys from the reeds
which grow on the marshes' fringe, posts for their roofs from tree trunks
uprooted in December storms, fretted screens for their low windows,
fencing for their yards, smooth handles for woodcutters' hatchets, frames
for the few faded pictures taken by an itinerant photographer who hasn't
been heard of since—
What haven't I done for them!

I have been sitting here since the autumn winds came,
outside my workshop in the dusty square,
listening to the ceaseless cries of the woodcutters in the woods,
thinking of the sighs of women whose names I have forgotten,
though I still remember their voices and can tell them apart,
who would lie back in the darkness of my shop
then resume their cheerful climb up to the woods to feed their men.

The tasselled gypsies passed through on their way to the distant ports
and I did not go with them.
The silk trader and his three boys came through
and I did not go with them.
The apple seller and his ancient mule,
and I did not go with them.

The white storks,
and I did not follow them.
The soldiers en route to the latest war,
and I did not walk with them.
The tax collectors and the field inspectors, the hunters and the men with
their chickens and herds, the young men on their way to the latest war,
and I did not go with them.
The sister-killer and the dead girl's seducer were followed by the deaf sister
who saw everything,
and I did not question her.
The pilgrims off to Mecca,
and I did not go with them.

The autumn winds came and the poplar leaves fell while I sat here
    outside my workshop in the dusty square,
counting the children and calling them by their mother's names,
listening to the shouts of the olive pickers on the low slopes
and to their muttering, returning late with their sparse harvest,
and to the coughing of those going to the dawn prayers, to their voices
roughened by sleep and cracked by their dry dreams.

The harvesters passed me
on their way to other men's fields in the northern plains,
and I did not go with them.
The hunters to the gazelle grounds,
and I did not go with them.
The builders to the stonecutters' hills,
and I did not follow them.
The funeral procession of the girl murdered by her brother,
and I did not walk behind them.

The survivors of fires in forests far away came here and slept in the square,
with their soot-covered faces and their reek of burnt grasses,

broken-hearted, standing at the bolted doors of the houses,
   the doors I made.
I heard one of their women weeping; she snivelled all night.
I haven't slept since.
   Sitting outside my workshop, I hear the weeping but cannot see the woman.

The gypsies returned from the ports having buried a woman and two boys
and in the square they set out
bracelets
and coloured beads
and bright cloth for wedding clothes.

The storks returned from the islands followed by their young.
The pilgrims returned from Mecca, sinless; in their packs shook
prayer beads
and coloured beads,
and the carpets shone across their saddles.
The soldiers returned from the latest war without spoils.
The tax collectors and inspectors returned without slaves or herds, and broke
down the doors of the houses and gathered the eggs before they could hatch.
The harvesters returned from the rich northern plains with stories and songs,
most of which I didn't believe, such as
the women there will run their hands over the bodies of the young men
toiling in the sun,
then make spells to bring those young men sleepwalking to their beds at night,
or that the oats there are piled higher than a horse's crop,
and other tall tales like these.

The woman, one of the survivors, and her broken heart
went on weaving out of her deep defeat a carpet, over the fences
and the children's dolls
and the hatchets' handles
and the nayys

51

and the kitchen shelves
and the faded pictures' frames.
With nicked and sooty fingers the carpet was crawling through the narrow alleys, up to the houses scattered along the only road to the woods, tapping on their bolted doors and shuttered windows, the fences round their yards, peering in at the broken bread on their tables.
The doors
and the windows
and the fences
and the tables
which I made with these hands of mine.

The wooden bell

The wooden bell that hangs in the dark is struck.
Is struck.
No one sees it
but it is struck.
No one is there
and the bell is struck.

It is struck on the front porch of the dream and in its shadowed corridors.

There is something priming itself in these shadows.

There is someone waiting.

Natures that never made it past the line are being shaped in vain.

A blind creature walks on air and collides with butterflies.

Laughter, too; not clear,
but laughter.

The wooden bell is struck.
It strikes the forehead of the man in his sixties who forgets, as usual, to duck
and wakes the losses worn out with remembering
and the losses about to begin.

A gust of wind springs suddenly from the red gum's crown and strikes it
and down the corridor flows the longing of the murdered wood.

The neighbour's daughter who spies on the man in his sixties rocks it
and the muffled creak of dead cane rushes the rooms.

A yellow butterfly with spotted wings arrives and it sways like a lantern.

A woman sighs in the darkness and her sigh perches on the fences
and the sills of the bright windows,
and out of the cane's absence is heard
a faint mizmar.

The cane trapped in the bell whispers over the river's surface,
wakes the drowned who were swept off by the flood,
and directs their dead eyes to their children
playing on the mountainside and collecting pebbles from the stream beds.

The wooden bell is struck and does not stop,
and far away, in the shade of the low shelters by the river, I hear it
swoop in like a swing full of frail hopes and glorious defeats.
It is struck here, as I fold away worthless marvels,
where strangers arrive with light coats and second-hand ideas,
and I hear it there, where I am young,
where on the riverbank dead children dry their clothes.

The silk road

The royal poinciana in the yard is what woke him that thundering night,
hard to forget,
in an unroofed room,
in a little inn,
in south Taiwan,
which was when he understood beyond a doubt that
that poem, Song of the Bowmen of Shu,
had taken place here in these wilds,
    and nowhere else.
The dead bowmen and their king were standing on the poem's colonnaded porch
outside the window
beneath the royal poinciana with
their dead hands,

and there was someone rapping on the pane.
He thought that it, the tree, was remembering him.
The wooden bell, too, was tolling in the hall.
He felt, strongly and almost instinctively,
that the bell was reciting names for the bowmen and their king,
and a name for the tree,
and that it was the hands of the merchants
that were rapping at his window,

the merchants' hands that, when all was done, went on
    fingering the silk road.
Sharp merchants,
bold merchants,
storytellers; merchants who lacked only time to be poets.

Drowned, they remember the horses

Here they are at last, the Arabs,
emerging from the forests and climbing from the riverbanks,
standing before the fences round the gardens
and the walls and the windbreaks
   leisurely constructed,
and offering up their daughters and their sons
like commentary on documented hadith, pretexts
over which they have no say,
followed by the drowned
in their overcoats bleached by salt, their eyes
pried open by the water,
and rising up over them the groan
of the holed boats.
They gaze at the villages
so far from their thickets of thorn,
and remember the saxaul, icon of their elegies.
There is another cry now, spilling over,
pushing them from the history books to the water,
from their robes and turbans tumbling
the linked chain of the jurists,
the stampede of the philosophers, the anecdotes of the wits,
and the ships flaming in the wake of the army of conquest
on its way to Andalus.

Here they are, the eloquent Arabs, falling
from the books of rhetoric, the marvels of the grammarians,

from expression's expanse and cramped meaning, with their blood
admixed by raiding, its purity surrendered to defeated nations, bewildered by
the rivers of Syria and the cities of Persia, dizzied by the villages of the Kurds
which hang like lanterns on the mountains.
The cunning Arabs, falling out of the cry without turning back to where they
left their elders on the minbars of mosques named for the Companions and
the Caliphs and the Commanders and the Great Imams, who scream out
after them over empty deserts,
and their jurists, still glossing death in terms of duty,
and their proselytizers, enumerating the virtues of the saints,
the descriptions of the houris,
the positions of congress,
to where their burnt offerings and feasts and temples trapped in the travelogues
    cry out,
and their marvels and manuscripts and silent statues
  in the cold museums of the north
    shed tears.
Here they are, the cruel Arabs with their gleaming eyes and muffled women,
their fingers turning their speech and spilling it over the bodies of the
northwomen, leaving on that pale skin marks and signs like runes
  difficult to decode or divine their purposes,
and their hands that breach paths to speech,
fingers that help them talk and laugh and weep.
Here are their voices,
filtering through the woods,
beating with damp wings over those sitting in squares
in remote villages
where men too old for work and the old women
who wear black for reasons unclear
still make the sign of the cross each time a drowned body comes to shore,
where the Muslims spared death keep screaming at their children

exhorting those whose bodies couldn't help them,
the women, the children,
to speak the shahadas.

Here they are, Arab louts: a burning desert dawn peeling back
off a great lamentation that drowns the world.

When We Lost the War

It happened during the mountain war

He never remembered that afternoon without a raincloud entering the house,
he never remembered it without a dog barking on the doorstep,
without the smell rising from a supper trying to simmer from the basement,
without there falling over his shoulders
the body of a young man heavy with death,
without hearing the sniper's shot,
without a woman
bundling over at the crossroads that he can see from the window.

At the bottom of the steps, a young man slain. One of them. Boots and gun.
On the doorstep, a dog. It seems afraid. It barks and does not stop.
And there was blood, and the smell of supper cooking, he couldn't tell what,
and people's voices coming from the basement: frightened voices rising and
turning through the rooms.
It wasn't clear where the young man was from. He was one of them. Clothes,
boots and gun. Or how he'd come to the stone two-storey house.
It wasn't possible to tell how long it had been since the sniper shot the woman
running across the junction.
But he picked him up. He was one of them. Watch, clothes, boots and gun.
He carried him from one floor to the next.
Carried him like he was remembering.
Picked him up to bring him with him into the raincloud of voices
and the vague smell of supper
rising from the basement and turning through the rooms.
Carried him to fetch him just a way away from his death
                 and because a reason for love was welling up from a time he found
hard to recall.

The sniper goes on firing at the dead woman on the asphalt.
The dead woman.
The dog, barking at the sniper.
The dead boy listening to the barking with a strange gratitude
          as he carries him from one floor to the other.
A house with two storeys, a basement, and a garden.

This happened in autumn,
during the mountain war that no one wants to remember,
the war in which many were killed
before it was covered over by other, more senseless, wars,
the war which they, whenever they dug to bury it,
would find another war down there taking shape,
the war which was dropped from memories
like an eighth daughter who should have been a son.
In his solitude, even he would forget those weeks and push them aside.
The war that was, to be exact,
   like a strain across his shoulders.
Only when he feels the weight of the dead body and the dog's bark
comes, when they come back, dead boy and dog, usually on September
mornings, when the dead woman appears, as though by arrangement,
does he return to his life as he knew it.

When we lost the war

Here we lost the war. We didn't lose, but mislaid it.
Put it down for a while beside the line of poplar trees in October.

Like orphans we are searching, said the soldier to his dead friend,
and his friend said: We left it here so we could pick olives.

Where is the war?
The soldiers' ghosts return before dawn;
they dig out the dark of the wells.

Where is the war? We were not beaten, but we lost it.

We were spared so we might love,
said the soldier to his dead friend,
and past them flapped a bird and clouds went by.

Don't despair, said a girl to the well as she gave its dark back.
Let it go.

We do not see you nor you see us

Your distant house cannot be seen from the plains.
Your blind house squats there, with its two windows that gaze to the valleys
    and do not see the plains
where the dead horses pasture silently
and the sound of slow chewing works through the hidden springs.

Maybe this is why at night you talk about the darkness
pouring into the rooms
and the trees that cling to the banks.

Maybe this is why at night we talk of the walls and corridors, secret and blind,
and the wars in which we have carried our slain enemies
as though remembering,
and the houses that the dead and missing tidy while we sleep.

Maybe this is why they talk, the inhabitants of the plains, through their
long nights, about the dead horses and the camels trapped in their dreams.
Your house we do not see, nor does it see us.
It walks towards the forest with two sightless windows and heavy curtains,
and a man stares into the dark and does not see the plain.

They didn't lack courage

They didn't lack courage or joy, those boys
who surrendered in the woods, who
were driven around in an open-topped truck then shot in the head
   on the slopes among the almonds.
They lacked neither beauty nor strength nor spirit.

You should have heard their laughter in the cold nights, surging out of the
foggy woods to our beds, trailing pine needles and damp cypress cones.

You should have heard their bawdy singing and the sadnesses like blemishes
that flawed its vigour and brought it to our warmed bodies within those walls.

You should have seen them on winter mornings, moving over the pine-covered
hills, gathering dewed cones and funghi shocked by thunder.

They did not lack courage, nor the glory that they earned and shared out
fairly with the novelists and public poets, the torchbearers and festival MCs,
the courtiers who compose songs of praise, who barter with loyalties, who
snipe from afar, the sentries in their mobile sentry boxes, the strutting cocks
who accompany the leader, the penpushers who come in once the fighting's
done and the ammunition's spent.

They didn't lack courage or joy,
those boys who raised their gunpowder-singed hands,
who held up their bloodied shirts on that October dawn,

who had fought on the rocky slopes of the southern highlands,
and the snowy foothills of Jebel al Sheikh,
and the hard ground of the high plains,
and the castle by Arnoun of which the singers sing.

65

During the mountain war they had carried down the bodies of their
enemies and set up gravestones on their graves,
recalling their faces whenever they spoke
and speaking their simple names in songs
that spread throughout the villages.

You should have heard their songs
that the villagers still listen to on winter nights,
remembering how their patrols went by on the cold mornings.
You should have heard those songs,
should have walked after the songs and followed the names
that now are mixed and muddled,
should not have turned till you came to the slopes of almonds,
that autumn long ago.

By force of habit

The soldier that the squad left in the garden,
the squad that the border guards left at the checkpoint,
the checkpoint that the occupation left at the crossing,
the occupation that the politician left in our lives,
the politician who was a soldier in the occupation,

the Merkava that the army left at the school,
the army that the war left in the city,
the war which the general left in the bedroom,
the general whom the peace left in our sleep,
the peace that was driving the Merkava,

still snipe at our heads
without orders,
just so,
by force of habit.

Going to Listen to My Father's Marvels

Going to listen to my father's marvels

Naked in your astonishment:
no fence, no knowledge, no shoulder to lean on,

only time, with its tests and tricks, time
which sends you back to the mirror each time,
like a rhyme scheme recurring,
like a gutter that drips in the dark,
when everything is hidden in the rhythm
that the gutter sends out from the dark.

Listening carefully to the rhythm, you touch in your listening
the bird and the cloud, the roof tiles
and wind, gravel and ditch,
the river's living mind and the fixations of its flow.
The rhythm is the great proof of things and the passion of the masks.

As though you were to find yourself standing, fully as you are,
in the mind of a poet who does not know you,
in the voice of a woman you cannot see, who once walked past you;
a simple woman, but who in some way and without meaning to,
stirred up the river's mist and hidden currents.

Skilled weaver, you will go against the wind,
against the years which, their work now done, sat down in the shade;
against the river, and against the boys who dream of maturing
without a sun,
without a journey.

Your neighbour who died last autumn will ask you,
Where to?
To listen to my father's marvels.

And the girl who loved you in a winter that never was asks,
Where to?
I left my mother's laughter on the balcony.

And a poet who resembles you, or who, to be precise, is you,
who just came in by boat, asks,
Where to?
To wake my beloved.

And a woman frowning as she darns your sock beneath a dim light asks,
Where to?
I follow the rainclouds.
And were they still raining there?
For many decades they have rained there.
It is coming, the rain, out of nowhere, out of Herod's dark signings.

The barbarians, my own

My enemies, my enemies who suddenly vanished, whom I,
                    when I woke, could not find
    where they are always hiding,
                    are gone.
                                        God,
where have those ghosts gone who would fill the night
    with whispering and fixations and doubt
        and hunting thoughts,
where the hay in the old dreams crumbles to dust
and strangers laugh in uncompleted poems?
I should have thought of them more, given them more cause and reason,
shown more interest in their efforts, encouraged them to stay, say, with
a gesture perhaps, or a touch of anger, or the head sadly bowed, a pause
as though affected, things like that.
It would have cost me nothing but have meant so much to them and
given them a reason to stay.
I should have fed them now and then so they could keep on with their
anxious breathing between the thorns and the stones, should have
nourished their panting breath left on the birds' nests and the leaves of
the hill shrubs that lead to my door.
They were more than just enemies, something more than that.
They were the barbarians, my own, by whom I overcame my boredom
and made a glory of my isolation.

The daughter of darkness

The woman who took me far from the springs
where the strangers and scroungers teem,
did not send me to the market
full of the unemployed and the ruler's men,
did not dispatch me to the oven
where the youth with the bared and sweating chest stands at the fire,
did not take me to the port where fishermen and fishmongers
sniff at the robes of the women who buy,
did not send me to pick figs
where the village boys and watchmen's sons
  come with their fizzing bodies.
I am the daughter of darkness, I said to the woman
resting her weary back against the door,
the woman who weeps whenever I say 'my mother' to the dark.

The voice of the well

How to guide you, stranger?
Your journey's end is far away and your roads impassable.

How will you embrace me, when my people have confined me in the dark?
I see you and you cannot see me.

How will you kiss me when you have no name
and I have no memories?

Stranger, how to follow you
when my father has forbidden me from looking north
and my mother's stoned me as she stones the birds?

We were spared love

And so, my love, we were spared love,
the picture of jasmine, the inadequacy of a picture in the park,
spared sleep beneath old songs, the hunt
for magic in drivel, icon of those who come out from the well
where eloquence is a road for those who've lost their way.

We were spared walking blind, guided by a window that does not see us,
from an obscure regret that will grip our sleeves at a fold in the silk,
from laughter whose like we never found in books.

We were spared fear,
a rose withering in the ledger of accounts,
spared a reason for the reason.

We were spared because we were born to go,
the going that does not see,
the going that does not stop.

Walking, through an excess of some boredom, or an anxiety.

We were spared so much
because the trains whistle in our sleep
as they pass, wreathed with their going, down the roads.
So wake, my love, 'there';
wake, my love, 'here'.
And wake.

We were spared so much and we were not picked.

A Muslim poet in Macedonia

The white woman who suddenly appeared in the hall said,
in something like a whisper,
I'm a Muslim poet.
It was as though she was telling a secret
or offering a confession both impossible to avoid and hard to hear.
Her chest, so close, gave out warm waves,
a frangible scent of almonds
as she put a poem in my hand, handwritten in their language there,
and before she vanished, murmured something like God willing. In Arabic,
as though Inshallah was a name she'd taken,
that kept her company, guarded her beauty with its fatal
surrender to the vicissitudes of time,
that could be called three times
to summon back the magic she'd left
    in the air in that hall
        one brief spell more.

Soon September

Soon September
will lay the sleep of plants and busy creatures at the door,
bringing summer's dust and food of figs and patience,
laying its eggs between the yards and the houses.

In the back kitchen that opens onto the garden
the scent of coffee and tobacco plays, where everything ended
in a rush, meaningless,
without regret
or commitment.

September will bark at the door, the door to the garden,
but I am sleeping, and September knows this,
and the door knows,
and the house.

And sleep knows this,
and the neighbour with the marvellous moustache, and the woman
visiting the neighbour with the marvellous moustache knows,
but she opens the door,
and the door opens.

Sleeping,
  sleeping
    and it is barking.

Do not open the gate to the dog. I know it:
it would always come when we were children, when the houses were
  that later left us, and the faces

that have not for so long been among us.
Leave it be, do not open the door
   so that the barking does not pass into my room
or touch the fruit in the oil painting.

Do not bark in the garden, behind the glass, at the poplars.

I find no sleep

I wake because of the dogs that bark in my memories,
I wake because of the war,
because of the fear that crawls behind the sandbags
and peers from the cracks,
and because we left the blankets beneath the rain,
and abandoned the boy from the north in the ditch
with his frightened eyes.

I wake because of longing
and regret.
I wake because of love
and the desire to thank something,
and because the singing which I would listen to in sleep was taken by the wind,
dragged off by the ants to their mysterious kingdoms.

Your extraordinary sleep and the slight incline of your head

Your extraordinary sleep and the slight incline of your head upon the pane,
the slight tremors of your upper lip,
tiredness in creases below your lids.

Day's purposes effortfully folded away,
and the constant fear of cold in the hand folded into the greatcoat's collar.

Your beauty is so good:
you scatter joy without favour.

Your heart is so good:
you let us remember you.

What a shame you sleep, can't see
this beauty sleeping on a seat in the night bus
heading for the suburbs.

Autumn stumbles in the hills

Nothing happens here,

nothing you could force into a letter or a conversation.
The east wind hasn't blown for weeks,
autumn stumbles in the hills;

you might expect it
but you can never be sure.

The sounds that would come by night, at midnight,
of people encountering a strange and unknown thing
have stilled completely.

Silence comes, and the reek of fires draw closer with every breath of wind.

A solitary car, wheels gone, caught on the foot of the hills
like a promise given rashly by the road.

Hope with its heart of grass

I write things my friends don't like,
footnotes that my neighbours, robbed by life
each passing day, skip by,
muffled texts that my companions in the cafe quite ignore,
poems no one loves,
preoccupied with absence and with loss.
I write my elegy to love and to the old names
dressed in metaphors that give no hint of elegy.
Hope alone. Hope, no other,
with its heart of grass,
desolate and obdurate,
pushing them to the light.

As you slice the bread for your supper

There is something that remembers you,
that thinks of you now as you slice bread for a late supper.
Say, Muscat,
where sailors come to the public park to dance at night,
young men from Salalah and Mirbat and Raysut in the south.

The narrow path paved with black stone
that takes you from White Bridge to Sheikh Ibn Arabi's tomb—
to be exact, the black stone itself,
then Damascus that surrounds it all.

The abandoned house in the backstreet in Jabal al Lweibdah in Amman;
its low window
gained by grass and vines.

The little bridge over the river in Lodève,
and the girl, too; her name, I think, Olivia.
Olivia's laugh.

Also, the basement rooms in Abbasid Square in Damascus,
the bed in the corner
and the dog, barking in the unfinished painting of a woman bathing,
the shoulder of the woman in the painting,

or that town in Colombia whose name I forget,
the town where Gabriel Garcia Marquez was born, which he later left,
where a plump Amerindian poet lives now,
and where the little inn is, with its cramped little rooms
by the river, whose name I also forget,
with its rooms without keys.

Do Not Call to Me With Your Wide Eyes

Who stands at the window

Standing at the window in these cold mountains where the north is everywhere,
he has his reasons, which occur, and his purposes, which gather,
because there, he is the unfinished painting in this perfection,
seeming in his incompleteness
   somehow heroic,
and also because he stands in the enchanted corridor, where to stand is like
enacting a mysterious profession,
as though he is responsible for Kawabata's women or for shepherding their
tangled destinies, for granting Arab names to the frail ghosts which he sketches
between the shadows and sends out from his solitude with a savant's slowness.
From his solitude he continues to let out threads of silk to add to those that
are climbing invisible steps, steps which in his preoccupation he forgets to
complete, that walk on carpets whose edges have frayed,
   that never arrive.
But he hears them echoing down the narrow passages of the mountain houses
and pushing beneath the low fences of the yards.

Standing at the window he has many reasons and purposes,
such as undressing the silence, continuing to listen
so that he might in a lucky moment pick out the distant prickle of grasses
unbending in the dark beneath the snow's thin crust.

Do not call to me with your wide eyes

I am not asleep. I am not there.
Do not call to me with your wide eyes; you will wake the forest.

In my dreams I walk barefooted,
talk with my dead friends and laugh
in a room washed up here by the war;
I cross the street with a child's quick wit,
and carry bread for my father who has come home for a holiday.

Do not call to me, I am thinking of you.
Do not wake me, I am dreaming of you.

Standing at the window: another scene

Blind poems

At night, while they sleep,
I write blind poems
and hold their hand
and we push on in the dark.

Nature

The woods are a cart of trees and the hills are horses that draw the cart.
The dark is a river that runs beyond the window and night is a lake.
You and I are are an uncertainty that pushes on, adrift
   and not arriving.

Strange trees came to the hills

By night, strange trees came to the hills.
The voices carried the thoughts of the darkness to the window.
The prophecy examines the houses
       and in the woods birds talk of migration.

Grass

The grass grew
in the long
drawn out screams
of the dead.

The cypresses and the darkness

The trees alone—the cypress,
the close-mouthed cypresses—
were—were we to want to be precise—
the ones who took it seriously: the night.

Soil and scratches

At times, like tonight, I wake exhausted
with soil and scratches on my hands:
the others' mistakes which I buried in the woods
so I could call their owners by their simple names
rise up from their darkness
and stand outside the window pane.

Didn't open my eyes

I woke. I didn't open my eyes. The dark was passing over me
and I heard the rain falling on the plants.
Then there was a small hole, stumbling in the dark, and a woman
whose breathing I heard but did not see.

Nothing happened

In any case
nothing happened.
The night went on its way
and uncertainty left the trace of a river in the dark.

A prophecy

The prophecy comes first. It descends
out of time and the walkers' dreams.

It arrives before the event. It has been here
since no one now remembers when, moves
in the shadows and the domes and the cold stoves,
is like a patient ambush
that has all the time.

Picture

I search, unsuccessfully, for that picture,
the picture which you, when I talk to you about it, don't remember.
A picture that did not happen,
but which now seems necessary and is hard to live without.

A chair

It is just a single chair crossing the road,
paint peeling as it gets up every morning to grow older.
The passers-by don't see it nor the scroungers,
nor do they see how on its frail wood
strangers might encounter the power of premonition.

I did not mean

I did not mean
when I stood at the the window this morning
to see the last poplar leaf fall.

As though you have everything done

You're dressed simply tonight
and your hands are held in your lap
as though you have everything done,
as though you have done it all.

Starched white shirt

A starched white shirt in the closet in the apartment opposite
left a line of white in the closet's darkness
as though it was a distant party,
dead figures laughing on a balcony.

Shiny black shoes come down the stairs

In the apartment opposite, before the mirror,
are a pair of shiny black shoes.
In the top corner of the mirror
is a creased photograph in black and white of a young woman
standing at the foot of the stairs.
The shiny black shoes come down the stairs without stopping;
the young woman at the foot of the stairs
looks into the eyes of an old man having his supper.
Each stair renews with each new step
beneath the click of heels and the flex
of the bewitching insteps of little feet.

Your hand

Thanks to your hand which was there,
frail and afraid but able to send a signal;
which was how I came from the metaphor to this hill country
which remembers you as though you were real.

I left my bags in the night

Dawn comes on.
It advances entire
as I hang back confused.
I left my bags in the night.

As you would want

I am
who saw you
as you long to be seen.

Notes

This compilation consists of poems from the following published works:

Lā shāmata tudillu 'ummī 'alayya (No birthmark to guide my mother to me; al-'ahliyya lil-Nashri wal-Tabā'ati, 2014)

Mushātun yunādūna 'ikhwatahum (Walking, they call their brothers; Bloomsbury Qatar Foundation Publishing, 2015)

Tahaddath 'ayyuhā al-gharīb, tahaddath (Speak, stranger, speak; Manshūrāt al-Mutawassit, 2019)

Ghurabā'u bi ma'ātifin khafīfatin (Strangers in light coats; Manshūrāt Multaqā al-Turuq, 2021)

Page 7 ✦ **Wadi Qelt** is a valley that runs for some 45 kilometres from East Jerusalem to West Jericho, an average of 250 metres below sea level. It is one of the sources of the River Jordan and some believe that Qelt is the Valley of the Shadow of Death mentioned in the Old Testament. Early Christians would take refuge from persecution in its many caves.

Page 13 ✦ 'the newborn girl buried alive': refers to a custom among the pre-Islamic Arab tribes which was condemned and proscribed by the Prophet and the Quran.

Page 41 ✦ 'the khamseen could come in': the khamseen are seasonal winds freighted with dust and sand.

Page 43 ✦ **Beit Jala** is a town adjacent to Bethlehem in the West Bank.

Page 55 ✦ 'the Bowmen of Shu': the title of a poem by Ezra Pound, which is based on a poem attributed to King Wen of Zhou, the eleventh-century nobleman, retrospectively honoured in some traditions as the founder of the Zhou (or Shu) Dynasty.

Page 57 ✦ 'to speak the shahadas': refer to the two shahadas, or testimonies of faith, the utterance of which are the first requirement for entering into Islam.

Page 63 ✦ **'Let it go'**: here the girl is singing the refrain of a popular song.

Page 87 ✦ 'for Kawabata's women': refers to the Japanese novelist Yasunari Kawabata who won the Nobel Prize for Literature in 1968.